Get Ready to Telecommute:
Planning for Success

D.H. Vincent

ISBN-13: 978-1512375831
ISBN-10: 1512375837

This book is dedicated to those who seek a freedom in their own work style and choices.

CONTENTS

INTRODUCTION

Gone are the days when office spaces are just within the walls of a commercial area.

Today, many small businesses, along the big ones, choose virtual offices and telecommuting for their employees. Going virtual is increasingly becoming a demand trend worldwide. There are real estate agents, marketing consultants, and language translators who run their businesses from home. Even those high-paying jobs such as web designers, software developers and even graphic designers prefer working remotely.

Why is telecommuting on the rise these days? Before we go into detail, let's have a short rundown of what a virtual office is. Investopedia noted that a virtual office is a business location that exists only in cyberspace. So if you work from home, coffee shop, or at a friend's house with the use of technology like a laptop and Internet, you're working from a virtual office. In other words, you're also a telecommuter.

Put differently, you can work from any location as long as you have all the right technology or tools. How can you be ready to work from home? That's for you to find out as this book includes all the tools you need in setting up a virtual office.

Going back, telecommuting is on the rise because of the ease it brings to many business owners and especially for startup companies. A virtual employer does not need to spend bucks for office rent or healthcare of every employee, for example. A virtual employee, on the other hand, does not have to worry about delays due to traffic going to work. However, there is more. A virtual office comes with many conveniences that you'll read later on.

Are you ready to become a successful telecommuter?

Chapter 1: Are You Ready?

Working from home is something many people wish to do. The main issue is that many have absolutely no clue how to start. Some might believe that not having a long commute to work is a good reason. Some might end up preparing for working from home, while not knowing they are on the incorrect path towards being productive. It would be absolute key to perceive that working in an offsite office and working from home are two completely different activities. We will study what precisely you need to do to be an effective, productive telecommuter.

Let's investigate the process of working from home so we can prosper and love our jobs. We can prepare you for a heightened type of victory. Please consider a few things one would think of before starting to telecommute. Before working from home, you need to evaluate and verify that telecommuting from home is a suitable direction for you.

Before working from home, it is beneficial to assess your natural choices. Then equate that against someone already working from home. You need to investigate everyone who is effectively doing what you want to accomplish. Then identify the areas that fit your own working style. That is a great beginning point. Here are questions you should go over:

- Do you manage time effectively?
- Are you able to prioritize your tasks?
- Are you self-motivated?

Ideally, your reply to the questions was "yes." Those choices are typical among those who work from home. You have promptly taken the initial step towards working from home!

Deciding to leave your corporate job is not a breeze. Setting up a virtual office is a drastic choice for some of, and many of us don't get as much when we have a stable job. But if it's your first time to work at home, I'm pretty sure this is not going to be so difficult. You're not alone in this journey. But before you put up your office sign, it would help to know the pros and cons first. This chapter will help you a lot in deciding whether you fit in a virtual office setting.

A virtual office is way more convenient than an executive suite. It's the number one reason why many people are choosing to run their offices virtually. Perhaps it's also one of your reasons for setting up one. These days, massive savings are possible because anyone can afford a typical business expense without breaking the bank. Just imagine how much it would cost to run a commercial office space.

Below is a more detailed explanation how a virtual office will give you more convenience than a commercial office. Listed below are the pros or advantages of having a virtual office, followed by its cons or disadvantages:

PROS FOR BECOMING A TELECOMMUTER

ENVIRONMENTAL BENEFITS

Many people often talk about the benefits of working from virtual office on the aspect of digital communication. There's the lower cost of expenditure and a better quality of life for many telecommuters. But we want to go through environmental benefits first, since this is one aspect of the society that's very important and often not discussed about in personal conversations.

Telecommuting is one way of "greening" the work environment. Working from home or from any remote location benefits the environment because there's no need to travel in cars or ride a bus or train to go to work. It can cut fuel usage by up to 2.3 million barrels of oil if 41 million Americans would telecommute once a week. That rough estimate was based on The Telework Coalition's report in 2011.

Besides cutting back fuel consumption, telecommuting also saves the environment by reducing pollution and sustaining energy. In TelCoa's Top 10 Reasons to Telework, four causes go to environmental and societal benefits while the other six are for the employee, employer, and the economy. According to TelCoa, telecommuting declines the aftereffects from or likelihood of natural disasters, pandemics, and terrorist events.

According to Flexjobs, telecommuting also has hidden benefits such as using less paper and storage space; eliminating energy consumption from office spaces; and cutting down travel associated with work. Just imagine how many trees we save by going paperless.

REDUCTION IN STRESS LEVELS

In research conducted by the Statistic Brain in July 2014, job pressure turned out as the number one cause of stress in the United States. The factors causing stress are tension between co-workers and boss and work overload. Nearly half of all respondents said that stress had a negative impact on their personal and professional lives. Job pressure was followed by money, health, relationships, and poor nutrition.

As a telecommuter, you can overcome job pressure because there's more opportunity to balance your work as well as your life. In an info-graphic by the CarInsurance.org, it showed that the average employee says their stress lessened by 25% by working remotely.

About three out of four respondents also said that they eat healthier when they work from home. In my case, I used to skip breakfast and ate lunch with food from the vending machine. In short, I didn't have a healthy lifestyle while working in a company a few years back. It feels happier to be at home where I have more choices of what to eat.

Besides, when you work from home, you don't have to stress out yourself with the financial burden of childcare costs or transportation.

MONETARY BENEFITS

Many businesses set up virtual offices because of budget reasons. Just imagine how much you can save on gas, business attire, and lunch outside. Basically, the three things you'll look for in a company are the salary, healthcare, and location. As a virtual worker, you have lesser or no transportation cost at all. Besides, if you have kids and need a babysitter, you make the choice to hire someone or use a day-care for a few days a week.

But monetary benefits aren't just for employees. Employers can save as much on rental, electricity and phone bill, average employee cost, furniture, devices, and healthcare for the employees.

The average rent for a 500 square foot office is more than $700 a month if you're in a small town. But if you choose to operate in a metro city, it can cost as much as $29,000 a month. With a virtual office, you can still reap the benefits of having an actual office for less. You have the flexibility to work anywhere. So if you think the coffee shop is the perfect place to work, you don't have to pay for the space. Just purchase a latte or a sandwich while taking advantage of the free Wi-Fi.

ENHANCED PRODUCTIVITY AND CREATIVITY

In a study conducted by uSamp, Sixty-seven percent of 1,000 professionals agreed that working remotely makes them more productive. You can work from anywhere or from any location, and you can gain higher productivity.

Based on the Telework Research Network, companies such as JD Edwards, AT&T and Compaq reported that their telecommuting employees were more productive than their office counterparts.

There are companies who allow their employees to work from home at least once a week. Jennifer Brower, an IT Professional said she loves Work from Home Fridays because she does not have to waste one and a half hour commuting.

In one study by Professor John Roberts and his team from Stanford Graduate School of Business, it turned out that employees worked four percent more efficiently. Besides, fewer employees quit since they're happier working from home. This is good news, not just for individuals, but also for companies, too.

WE BECOME TECH-SAVVY

As virtual workers, we become more knowledgeable with technology and software that we use every day. We really have to be aware of the technology we have unless we have somebody else to fix these things for us. Because there's the Internet, we can definitely Google everything we need to know, including some troubleshooting on a device issue.

FLEXIBILITY

One of the reasons why many people leave their corporate jobs for a virtual business is the flexibility it gives them. I know a lot of work-at-home buddies who work when they want to and not so much when they don't want to. I, myself, enjoy this perk of working from home. I also get to choose the people I work for, and I must say that it is a great advantage of being a virtual worker.

Working from home is a win-win situation. Here's an example why. My niece worked as a sales representative in another city. Unfortunately, she didn't have the opportunity to witness all of her child's milestones. She didn't make it on her daughter's first day of school. The mother, of course, feels sorry for her daughter. I know many working moms or dads who have this kind of heartbreak. But now that my niece has taken her work home, she has more time to spend with her family. The results are amazing—she was able to carry on her interests outside her work while being there for her children.

As a mom, she understands how her kids benefit now that she works from home. She can still pursue her passion, which is writing, while she can look after the kids. Just imagine how much she saves on childcare. Plus, it gives us a better quality of life. As a mom, it's nice that she gets to witness her children's milestones.

On a personal note, I'm happier for not wasting so much time commuting to work. Personally, I had a hard time commuting to work a few years back. I spent three hours a day commuting to and from work. Not to mention the hours I spent preparing for work. I had to decide what to wear. Sometimes, I did not even have a choice but to leave with my hair still damp. An average American spends more than 24 minutes each way going to work. In Toronto, the average time is 32 minutes. My commute was three hours! I certainly could use that three hours doing something I enjoy like sleeping in and taking time to relax.

CONS OF BEING A TELECOMMUTER

Working in a virtual office or from anywhere has its advantages, but look out! It also has some drawbacks. However, you can solve these stumbling blocks along the way, and I have also come up with tips and pieces of advice.

Low Communication Efficiency

There is a lack of face-to-face communication in a virtual office, and that's why mishaps and confusions can happen. As they say, a face-to-face interaction is still the best in spite of having email, phone calls, and instant messaging. A face-to-face interaction makes way for lasting business relationships. Some people can't find time for this kind of interaction, though.

Most of us rely on video conferencing these days, which is reasonable. It's more convenient, you get to see nonverbal cues, and it's almost as effective as a face-to-face interaction. But what seems to be missing with a video conference is the shared presence of the surroundings. Around 90 percent of our communication is made up of body language and signals like yawning. Face-to-face interaction makes it easier for us to know if the other party is interested or not.

Video conferencing can make business meetings effective, but only to a certain point. It can make you feel isolated sometimes. In case you feel isolated at home, you can work from a coffee shop or where there are other people around. This way, you'll guarantee a more social atmosphere.

TIME DIFFERENCE

Working with global clients? Differences in time zone are one thing many employees face. Even an hour or two difference in time can be challenging to manage. Let's say it is 9 am in Toronto and you have to talk with a client urgently. You are from Seattle where it's only 6am. How will you manage that? It only means you will have to adjust your schedule wisely for you to make things easier for you and for your client.

If you need a meeting planner but find it difficult because your client has a different time zone, you may try the World Clock Meeting Planner. Google Calendar also has an option to show additional time zones on your calendar. Or if you have a distributed team working in different time zones, you might need to experiment on strategies to keep working going. It also helps to know your colleague's time zones. Time Zone Converter, Gmail Time Zone Tricks and World Time Zone are just some of the free web tools for managing time differences.

LOSS OF EFFICIENCY

Employees can also lose their motivation, especially if there is no proper management practices in place. As I said earlier, virtual workers work when they want to. The statistics can prove this one as true. Almost half of American professionals say it's hard to maintain productivity when working from home.

For one to be more effective working from home, it helps to come up with some strategies. There are the kids, the phone, the doorbell, the social network, and the household chores. Many of us chime on the subject of "distraction." Here are some distraction-free tips from people who also work from home:

➢ Use cloud storage for your files. Dropbox and Google Drive are two of the most commonly used options. Storing your files on cloud makes it easy for you to access your files anywhere. Whenever I'm on the go and there's a situation when I need to submit something because the client wants the file again, I just look at my Dropbox.

➢ Avoid drop-in visitors. Sometimes, even our friends have this negative perception that we're just at home so it's okay to drop by anytime they want. In case your friends happen to stop by, politely tell them you're working. Or better, have some chit-chat time with your friends during weekends. Take advantage of Skype for this matter. This way, you won't feel so isolated. Setting aside time for your friends is a good way of balancing your personal life and your career. But the most important thing in here: you have to let them know when you work.

➢ Create a comfy workspace. Do you love your workplace? Most of us don't have a dedicated office space. It won't cost you an arm and leg to have one. Many home-based workers say having a home office makes them more productive. Plus, it will make you feel professional. Sometimes, getting things done also depends on the environment you work on.

NEGATIVE PERCEPTIONS

Using your home address as your business address can be complicated for many reasons. People might have negative perceptions like if your company is real or if you'll still be running a business there after several months.

If your client worries that you're going to work three hours and then vanish, you might mention your availability on your job description and to clients. Besides, it's easy for people to think that you're not working. In Ryan Gibson's post in Generation Y, he mentioned that his neighbors' kids thought that he was unemployed. Sometimes, I have that same thinking. Do other people see me lazy because they think I'm not working? Oh, I guess I should stop thinking too much about what other people think of me.

LESS OPPORTUNITY FOR BREAKTHROUGH INNOVATIONS

Collaboration and interaction are very essential to any successful business. Yes, video conferencing can let you brainstorm with others, but interacting in person is better. If it's not possible to have face-to-face interactions, find a community of freelancers online. Odesk, Elance, and FreelanceSwitch are some of the sites where you can find thousands of freelancers. They can help you brainstorm and hone your ideas.

In this case, Yahoo!'s CEO Marissa Mayer banned their employees from working from home. There are only two choices: quit their jobs or move from home to Yahoo's nearest office. This can be annoying for some professionals who work at their best at home, but Yahoo was right for saying this:

"To become the absolute best place to work, communication and collaboration will be important, so we need to be working side-by-side. That is why it is critical that we are all present in our offices."

The note was from the company's human resources chief Jackie Reses. Michael Katz, an ex-Yahoo and a former ad tech executive supports this move. He says the value in human interaction is greater collective wisdom as a result of improved communication and collaboration.

TRUST ISSUES

From an employer's point of view, it's a challenge to motivate employees to work. Staying motivated at home is not a piece of cake, especially if you're working on a project you don't like. That's why they say working from home is problematic at times.

STAYING ORGANIZED

Ironically, it's easier to organize in a traditional office than in your office at home. During the first year of my home-based job, I thought I was going to be more productive. Most of the time, yes, I am more productive; however, juggling household errands and work is no piece of cake.

LESS CAMARADERIE

Working from home can become quickly mundane. It can be so lonely especially if you're used to a traditional work environment. Some even find it isolating to work from home. Somehow, it's true since there's the reduced ability of sharing information through face-to-face communication. There's less social interaction when you work in a remote area. But this issue can be solved by having regular video conferences, work from the local coffee shop, or, better yet, take a trip to the beach and work.

HERE ARE SOME TIPS TO GET YOU OFF THE GROUND:

-- ESTABLISH WORK ROUTINES

No matter how much you prepare to work from home, it is undeniable that establishing work routines would be a must right out of the gate. That is why it makes sense to practice establishing work routines, before you get into the central focus of the things you need to make happen.

-- BLOCK OUT DISTRACTIONS

A necessary step in laying the groundwork that is required to work from home involves blocking out distractions. When you block out distractions, it trains you to continually improve your productivity and mental state.

-- ORGANIZE SCHEDULE AND WORKSPACE

Organizing schedule and workspace is a no-brainer. You likely already perceive that you need to organize your schedule and workspace in order to work from home. Individuals who are unable do so, will surely face trouble with meeting deadlines and producing quality work.

Now that you perceive that you need to be in the appropriate mindset to work from home, we will investigate certain preliminary habits that someone working from home would already be doing. Use that opportunity to draw in these habits into your decisions because that will make preparing to work from home easier.

Working from home involves slightly more than getting up one morning to say, "Wow, I need to work from home." Possibly that is the first step. However, to gain a bit of benefit in working your plan, you should first invest mentally.

D.H. Vincent

Chapter 2: Is Working From Home Right for You?

Most people who choose to work from home are really strong-willed. There are several qualities in life which cannot be faked. You cannot fake a job interview or the outcome of finals in school. Likewise, you cannot fake working from home. You simply cannot work from home without a little foresight. Telecommuting from home involves someone to be effectual and strong-willed. It involves vigilant planning.

When you are planning your behaviors to work from home, make sure that you do not start the day without a plan. Additionally, do not try to put off your morning ritual. Preparation involves time and it must not be rushed. By darting through the period of preparation, you would not truly be training, and it can be concluded that you faked your way through the steps. Doing it the appropriate way would allow you to maintain longevity toward your results.

Working from home ought to be quite stimulating and allows a sense of accomplishment that you will treasure and improve upon every day. Working from home is a challenge. Whether you could be inexperienced or are totally experienced, there are logical pros and cons of working from home which we discussed in Chapter 1.

There are more advantages of working from home and the top one would be that it will allow you a sense of pride and accomplishment. Telecommuting from home is a life-changing activity. Working from home would be something that may constantly remind you of your commitment to personal freedom and allow you a sense of fulfillment for just trying.

A different great benefit of working from home would be that it perfects your preparation skills because you have to prepare how you will move forward to realize a new working environment. So once you choose to work from home, you may learn a lot about planning as well as staying focused.

There are undeniable results to working from home. It is certainly not as effortless as it sounds. There can be certain limitations that you possibly need to rise above, like the investment of time required to plan. You need to allow yourself time, and make a total commitment. You may have to plan in segments. Devotion as well as sincere effort will ultimately guide you to discover the value of telecommuting.

This would allow you some insight to establish if working from home would be ideal for you. Without a doubt, working from home definitely needs someone to be motivated, creative, and energetic. When you regard yourself as the kind of person with these characteristics, you may be completely prepared.

The most critical thing to be aware of would be there are no shortcuts. Most people who have recently worked from home perceive how much commitment is needed. You need to listen to your internal voice, which will lead you through the steps required to be prosperous.

When you telecommute, there are usually some key activities that you have to accomplish. You have to set up work space, arrange a daily work schedule, and use productivity tools. Those three activities do not just help individuals out with working from home, they more importantly bring other direct benefits to life. Telecommuting from home would be something which has made countless men and women everywhere feel better about themselves.

Most people who were setting up work space could identify slight transformations in their inner well-being. Those people more importantly feel primed to tackle more things in life. Priming in advance allows you to be stronger than what you had been before. This allows you to complete more than you could do before, and not lose energy as easily. That all benefits you, and that more importantly serves you in your natural decisions.

Individuals arrange a daily work schedule while they plan to work from home. Evidently, arranging a daily work schedule has various results aside from solely spending less time on work and more time with family or friends and meeting short- and long-term goals. You would also find that you can have less stress to meet deadlines at last minute. All this will make you become better on an everyday basis.

Telecommuting from home also results in finishing daily work in fewer hours. It results from using productivity tools, especially spanned over a longer period of time. Furthermore, that brings tons of additional results. For example, you will meet deadlines easier and quicker. Furthermore you will have less job stress.

Working from home would be an activity where anyone can constantly better themselves through the period of preparation. While training and planning can take some time, this means that you would probably have to work constantly for a period of time. Working from home will make you be stronger and better primed for your everyday challenges.

Understand you aren't the only person in the world who has the aspiration of working from home. Really, there are many men and women everywhere who hope to telecommute. Some will be successful; others will not. The reality is that only a small percentage of people will seriously take the plunge and accomplish it to a high degree.

So then, just what do we know? Essentially, we know working from home is no effortless task. Working from home definitely needs you to be effectual, dynamic, as well as energetic. Now we will move on to just what you truly have to do to make it happen.

If you assess people who have done well in working from home either recently or in the past, you will find something similar among the people who have done well. They saw what was required before starting, and they knew what type of person is likely to succeed. When you learn what type of personality is necessary to work from home, there is nothing that will block the trail between you and your success!

Working from home has a tangible aspect to it. Any activity for which you plan beforehand will end with a beneficial result. You will find the strength and your mind will lead you to your objective.

You have determined whether or not you are dynamic once you were asked: Are you able to prioritize your tasks? Congratulations for making it this far, because that means you clearly have not surrendered. It is a huge difference between doing something and desiring to do it.

You've already begun a major step for being primed to work from home. Many people fail for good reason. They simply did not perceive what they would be getting themselves into. Working from home is that one thing in life that requires you to be entirely focused and prepared. Through looking ahead and making sure you are the right fit for telecommuting, you are taking the initial step toward being prepared.

You may want to check whether you have the initiative it takes to do it. Do you maintain a motivated attitude? It would be an integral part of the formula that every individual who expects to work from home successfully needs, or else telecommuting from home will be overwhelmingly tough, if not impossible.

Also consider that setting up work space is certain to impact to your success. Your mind might try convincing you that working from home could be rather tough or is certainly not worth the effort, but through setting up work space and concentrating on your goals, you can do it! Let's determine how we will now plan for working from home!

Chapter 3: Virtual Office Expenses

For most people, home is the perfect place to set up an office. But for businesses which require collaborating in person or have clients come to see products, a workspace is necessary. If you wish to have all those facilities of a real virtual office on your own space, here it is:

OFFICE DESTINATION

A business address is necessary for a business to look more professional. But having an office is one of the biggest expenditures of a business. Add the equipment, electricity, and other additions like Internet and telephone connections, that would be a huge amount of money. So if you don't want to put all your investment on renting an office space, and if you don't really need one (like researchers, writers, and designers), your home could be the best office destination. Besides, you're not alone because more than 2.8 million workers choose home as the perfect work destination. Here are some things you can do to comply with Internal Revenue Service (IRS) requirements, from Intuit website:

1. Once you picked a portion of your room as your home office, be sure that the personal spaces are separate from your business space.

2. The home office must be the primary area where you conduct your business.

3. Only get decorative items appropriate for your home office.

4. Your desk, computer, and cabinet should all be part of your office. If you have a shipping area, it should be there as well.

5. You may want to rent a post office box instead of using your own home address.

Want more tips to reduce your taxes? According to Keith Hall, President and Chief Executive at the National Association for the Self-Employed, says to find what percent your home office will be used. Use that measurement to determine the business part of expenses like home repairs and mortgage interest. Your home can either be a productive or a disruptive place. It helps to set aside a dedicated work area that includes some rules you make about being distracted. This way, it still feels like you're working in an office, and you'll be in the mindset of productive work.

FURNITURE FOR YOUR OFFICE SPACE

Aside from a desk space, you also need an expense for office supplies such as storage boxes and desk organizers. Besides Ikea, there are other stores selling quality furniture for less. Wal-Mart sells office desks and task chairs for less than $150.

If you want to save money, I would suggest you look for cheap office furniture near you instead of buying new. There are tons of places that sell used office furniture in good condition. Some stores even sell interesting vintage pieces and elegant pieces at a reasonable price. Check out eBay or Craigslist or even garage sales to find economical office furniture.

DESKTOP/LAPTOP

Not so long ago, small businesses preferred using a desktop over a laptop. Both devices have their advantages. Some people like a desktop because they grew up using a desktop. It also has the ergonomic advantage with its big screen and full-size keyboard. Attaching two extra monitors allows for more applications to be seen. On the other hand, laptops are portable and only require little electricity. There are drawbacks too. For example, a desktop computer is easier to repair than a laptop because it's easy to open a desktop PC.

When it comes to issues of upgrade options, a desktop can take more Random Access Memory (RAM) than a laptop. A 15-inch MacBook Pro costs around $1,200. Most professionals prefer an Apple laptop because of its lightweight, productive, and retina screen features, but there are other budget laptops out there with good quality. Multiple monitors are available for both types of computers.

Further, deciding which one to buy will also depend on its purpose. For programmers, screen size and comfort of a keyboard are two of the most essential factors to consider in buying a laptop. Dell, Lenovo, and Asus are just some of the brands out there that you can try. There's a huge list of laptops on the market and choosing one will still depend on the comfort it gives the user. On the other hand, web developers have different preferences. Dell also has their developer edition, along with Sony Vaio, and Samsung. Do your research when buying a laptop or a desktop because it's going to be one of the biggest purchases you'll have on your home office.

In case you can't afford a separate computer, just make sure you estimate the time you spend on your family computer and use that number to identify your business hours.

SOFTWARE AND PROGRAMS

To make your job easier, install the latest software as well as programs on your computer. In case you don't have someone to coordinate with virtual office software, here are some links to some of the most popular software:

Word Processor- if you're a MAC user, you're familiar with NeoOffice as a free option and a Nisus Writer Pro for the paid version. But you can still take advantage of Microsoft Word which you can buy from the Microsoft website. If you do coding, TextWrangler and BBEdit are some of the great options. TextWrangler features web authoring and software development tools. For online word processors, there are Google Docs, iWork for iCloud, and AJAX Write.

Anti-virus software- The good news for MAC users is that you don't need to install an anti-virus in an Apple computer. There is anti-virus software for Apple but they're not very valuable. The best way to get rid of malware on your MAC is to always keep the system software up to date. For Windows 7, Microsoft Security Essentials, Avast, and NOD32 from Eset are some of the popular choices.

Email program- a dedicated email is essential for business purposes. For me, Google Mail's features are easy to use and business-appropriate due to its simple layout. If you're not used to Gmail, you may check out the Ultimate Guide to Gmail from the Make Use Of website.

Computer maintenance utility- for cleaning your registries, there's Wise Registry Cleaner. For system cleaning, there are CCleaner 4.02.4115.

Printer and printing accessories

If your intent is to go paperless, you may not need a printer at all. But in case you hardly need one for business purposes, buy a printer which works as an "all in one". Find one that could work as a copier, a scanner, and a fax machine. A multifunction computer at Amazon is around $350.

Office Tools

The number one reason why many virtual offices fail is due to complicated tools. There are possibilities of network slowdown and lack of high speed. Then there are apps which are designed to make us productive but not user-friendly enough. So it's better to choose which ones to use for your virtual office. With the right tools, working in a cyber space can be as effective as a traditional office. Here are the essential tools as well as tips to keep your tool at its best:

AN EXCELLENT INTERNET CONNECTIVITY

A stable wireless Internet connection has been a must since our productivity depends on this aspect. Otherwise, it will be hard for you to work seamlessly. Here are 10 ways to make your internet connection faster:

Run a speed test. Basically, a speed test won't show you everything but it can be a useful diagnostic tool. Speedtest.net works by measuring your broadband performance.

Update your browser. Check if your current browser is up to date. The reason for this is that programmers constantly update them and improve their performance. Besides, there are browser-based tools that you make use of. For example, there's WriteSpace which is accessible when you're using Chrome. Below are the latest versions of some commonly used Internet browsers

- ➢ Mozilla Firefox 33.0
- ➢ Internet Explorer 11
- ➢ Safari 5.1.7
- ➢ Google Chrome 39.0

Get rid of viruses. Always prefer Safe Mode with Networking when running Windows. This way, you can make sure malware isn't loaded when you visit a site. Also avoid clicking on everything. There are pop up ads that mimic the design of some anti-virus software. You have to be aware of these ads since they could bring virus or Trojans on your computer. If you want to get rid of banner ads and pop up banners, install an add blocker on your browser. It can help eliminate unnecessary ads which add clutter to various pages. One more thing, Delete temporary Internet data. Fix a slow

Internet connection by deleting browser history. Remember to clear your cache at least once a week.

Set a network password. Using the default password is an unpleasant idea because hackers or anyone else can easily track it down on the router manufacturer's website. Do you have a hard time changing your network password? Below are some suggestions how:

- ➤ How to change wireless network password of a Linksys router
- ➤ How to change a D-Link wireless password

Use a wireless repeater. It works by being the bridge between a router and connected devices. A wireless repeater is a stand-alone unit unlike a wireless booster which refers to an upgrade around the modem itself. It costs around $70-$400. But if you don't want to spend some more for a wireless repeater, you can do some DIY project using your old router. Lifehacker features an article on how to turn your old router into a range-boosting Wi-Fi repeater.

Relocate your wireless router. One of the simplest changes to increase your Internet speed is by relocating your router. You may also buy an access point. It helps boost the signal especially when you place it upstairs.

Check the weather. Does increment weather have something to do with slower Internet? Yes, storms and heavy rains could affect your broadband's performance. Perhaps it's due to higher demand of Internet usage since most of us would rather stay inside than hang out. And what do we often do on these days? Most of us enjoy watching movies from gadgets, playing video games, or checking our social media accounts.

Clean up your hard disk. Install a CCleaner which works by protecting your privacy online while making your computer faster. It can be installed on a PC, in an Android device, or a MAC. Your PC also has a Disk Cleanup feature which can be found on

Accessories. Just go to All Programs, select Accessories, and then go to System Tools.

Close unnecessary programs. Sometimes, the problem is not on the Internet. There are background programs that could make your computer slow. You may check out some advanced free system boosting tools which automatically closes unnecessary tools. Or go to your Task Manager to check which applications are running.

VIRTUAL COMMUNICATION TOOLS

Google+ Hangouts is great for video conferencing. Aside from Hangouts, WebEx, GoToMeeting, and iMeet are some of web conferencing tools to try. GoToMeeting is more stable than Google Hangouts and Skype but it only allows six video feeds.

If you want high-end video conferencing tools, try Cisco Teleconference or Logitech Lifesize. In case you need to hold meetings, Hangouts also comes with this feature. These days, it is also available for Apple devices. Skype is also a nice option for instant chatting and video conferencing.

A GOOD WORKING COMPUTER

Modern technology is evolving. Before computers, word processing was done by hand. Now that we live in a robotic age, almost all kinds of jobs require a computer. Yes, a computer. But this time, you'll need a real good one since it's going to mean a lot to your business. I remember working on a very slow computer, and to my exhaustion, I ended up writing down my ideas on a paper instead. At some point in life, you'll also realize that a pen is mightier than a laptop.

A good computer doesn't really have to be the most expensive in the market. It should be a combination of functionality and affordability. There are so many you can choose from—laptop, desktop, or tablet which can be connected to a keyboard. Of all these choices, I prefer a laptop simply because I can bring it anywhere and a desktop with three monitors. I haven't tried using hybrid laptops, but I guess they're a good option if you want an interchangeable device.

FILE SHARING

For sharing files, there's Dropbox, Microsoft SkyDrive, and Google Drive. I like that Dropbox has a free version which lets you store up to 2GB of files. If you want more space, you can choose from Dropbox Pro and Dropbox for Business. SharePoint Online is another Microsoft product which comes in different plans. If you want one with a free trial version, you can check out Onehub.

PHONE LINE

This oldie but goodie tool may or may not be adequate for your home office. I say so, because that would depend on the kind of job or business you have. For example, there are some home-based call center jobs that will require you to have a separate phone line. There are some who don't and would allow you to use Skype or Google Voice for the calls.

Either way, you have to think about having a dedicated phone line for business. The IRS could legitimize your home office because of a work line. For that reason, just consider a cell phone for your business.

COLLABORATION TOOLS

In case you need to collaborate with more than one or two people, it helps to have a central hub where you can share ideas. Here are some collaboration tools you can install:

➤ Redbooth- lets you manage projects, share files, communicate with teammates, and assign tasks.
➤ ActiveCollab- works as a project and task management
➤ Blackboard Collaborate- its latest version comes with a built-in audio conferencing. It's a nice try for online teaching and brainstorming.

➢ Only Office (formerly Teamlab)- also features a calendar for you to easily track your team's work.

➢ Lighthouse- nice tool for seeing the status of projects in one overview.

➢ Morally- it looks like a digital sticky note that you can share with the team.

WORK MANAGEMENT SOFTWARE/APP

Wrike is widely held software for virtual collaborations. It works by gathering all projects and tasks in the system while making it easy to share one's work for a company or individual. Proofhub is another collaboration tool, but it's available online.

Occasionally, people believe it could be cost prohibitive to work from home. It's actually the opposite. You could completely telecommute from home for virtually nothing. When you are seeking to telecommute from home, the key thing to make happen would be to start with a clear mind. In other words, eliminate from your mind all preconceived notions of whatever the planning phase for working from home is supposed to be like.

Rather, devote your effort on the preparation. Also consider, setting up work space, arranging a daily work schedule, and using productivity tools should be integral tips to get primed for working from home without needing to go into debt. Most timesaving apps are reasonably priced and have lifetime usage benefits. Create separate lists of your tasks for work and for household chores. This works especially for moms. If you want to master your to-do list, it is important that you find a good balance between working and being mom.

Investing additional money would certainly not make you work from home better. Therefore, do not go searching for stores to blow your money on technology gadgets when you telecommute from home. I say this, but be sure to have a good dependable laptop or computer.

Chew gum. They say chewing gum boosts productivity. Some say it is just a myth. But one study in St. Lawrence University in New York suggested that chewing gum has positive cognitive effects. Whether it is proven to boost productivity or not, chew a stick and try it.

Place a plant near your desk. Plants, when placed strategically, raises alertness by up to 70%. Some good choices are areca palms, which humidifies naturally; variegated snake plant, which purifies the air; and lemon balm which elevates the mood .Once again, there are a ton of economical alternatives to achieve the final goals to steer you through working from home comfortable. Before these alternatives were convenient, people had been working from home without all the streamers and balloons which follow the more cost prohibitive alternatives.

The greatest suggestion is surely to maintain your main objective as the main priority. More precisely, setting up work space, arranging a daily work schedule as well as using productivity tools are areas you may want to focus on in the early weeks of your telecommuting. During the time you really look at your behavior, it is increasingly easier to identify when you are wasting money for stuff you don't need.

Setting up work space does not require a ton of money. The aspiration would be to enjoy a work space that promotes productivity, and that ought to be realized with minimal spending because it really does not need to be cost prohibitive. The reason you need to focus on arranging a daily work schedule would be so you can spend less time on work and more time with family or friends. Again, that does not require a ton of spending to achieve.

Conclusively, devote some effort on arranging a daily work schedule, as well as how you ought to use productivity tools properly. Do not willingly allow yourself to get swamped by options which encourage excessive spending. Remember, there are more effective alternatives available and productivity tools that are low in cost.

Regardless, you need to usually choose where you spend your paycheck through thinking of your key aspiration of working from home. Your feelings will play a large role when looking at your money. You might be searching for an easy, minimalist method to work from home. Through recognizing this, you ought to make a lot of progress toward your aspiration.

D.H. Vincent

Chapter 4: The Daily Grind

Working from home might not be something which you decide to do on a day-to-day basis, but if you assess the effects of working from home, you might blend that in your work process. The truth is that working from home brings side effects which will benefit other aspects of life.

Do you remember being asked the following?

- Do you manage time effectively?
- Are you able to prioritize your tasks?
- Are you self-motivated?

Along with looking at your lifestyle, these questions are also seeking to analyze your capabilities and desires. So in the event you answered yes to these questions, there would be an implication of what is important to you.

Certainly, no one will ever say working from home is effortless. It is undeniable that you have to be effectual as well as dynamic to even try working from home. Just keep in mind that fulfilling activities take effort and commitment. If living out great successes was as effortless as snapping your fingers, everyone might be doing it.

The greatest thing about working from home would be the effectual quality that would be necessary to succeed which will make its way in other aspects of life. This would help you to be a more effectual person overall. When you telecommute from home, you are training yourself for what is to follow. Success. It would be just one of the great things of working from home.

Working from home helps you in other areas of your life. That would be undeniable once you start telecommuting from home. Things such as establishing work routines, blocking out distractions, as well as organizing schedule and workspace all require skills which you may use in other areas of your life. Working from home provides many useful skills that are easily transferrable to all aspects of your life.

When you assess working from home as a lifestyle as opposed to a goal, you will find it effortless to adopt the habits that enhances your success. The adjustment in your regimen has a relevant purpose beyond accomplishing a single objective.

One may have a strong desire to work from home, or it may be that you are forced to do so. Either way, telecommuting can and will give you more choices in how to spend your time.

Those who are devoted to the overall goals will find working from home completely gratifying. Congratulations for taking that step toward this lifestyle/

We discussed a few of the assorted habits that someone who expects to work from home ought to think of carrying out. Now that you have understood the choices of someone desiring to work from home, the probability is that some choices are mixed into your everyday decisions already. You ought to investigate how you can cultivate these tendencies into a bigger part of your behaviors. This will make the change to working from home an easy evolution.

Regardless, preparing to realize the utmost goal will require you to adhere to a few transformations in your decisions. Your acceptance to transforming yourself will be the determining factor in how swiftly you accomplish your calling.

Are you primed to establish work routines? Are you primed to block out distractions and organizing schedule and workspace? Those are just certain habits to prepare you for the quest of working from home. If that sounds distressing, do not agonize. I have a few tips related to accomplishing your goals.

DO NOT DART THROUGH THE PREPARATION STAGES.

Occasionally, it may appear that the preparation stages may be skipped. Conceivably, you might believe you may flourish without carrying out things like establishing work routines. There may probably come a time after beginning the preparation of working from home where you would face a task such as setting up work space. If you finish the preparation stages beforehand, you will face a much easier time accomplishing your goals.

Investing a calculated period of time solely to focus on the little things would be ideal. It would cause the latter strides of your quest to be smoother. Conclusively, you will be fully primed to work from home after the preparation has begun.

DO NOT CALL IT QUITS IF YOU FAIL PREPARING.

However critical your effort might be, expect imperfections. Rather than pursuing perfection, try following the preparation stages the best you can. That would allow you a safeguard to mess up the steps periodically. If you anticipate stumbling from perfection periodically, that will prevent you from surrendering while you waver from using the steps of working from home effectively.

INVEST IN A FAST INTERNET SERVICE. SPENDING MORE ON THIS WILL REAP YOU PRODUCTIVITY BENEFITS.

It may look like an undeniable thing to accomplish while you are preparing to work from home. Nonetheless, it is surprising how some people fail getting the best service beforehand. This would be an easy tip to try. Do not make the biggest mistake of darting through these essential preparations.

TRY THE EAT-THE-FROG TECHNIQUE

Where the frog symbolizes the most unwanted task you have for that day. Henry Paulson, a businessman and author, said that the first thing he did every morning was the thing he was dreading the most that day—eating the frog.

Whether you're trying to accomplish a material aspiration or a critical part of the formula which involves more creative energy, your intellect leads what you do. That would be why, it would be critical to prepare yourself for the tasks at hand. When the mind is equipped toward the tasks at hand, that results in carrying out the work faster. Whatever we accomplish starts with a hope. Follow some simple advice, and the quest to work from home will be completely underway.

WHEN YOU THINK OF GIVING UP, DO NOT.

It would be natural to get discouraged while things become tough. If working from home was effortless, everyone would be doing it. The truth would be that working from home involves some effort and calculated action. The benefits could be really fulfilling. Even if you might want to call it quits while things get tough, do not. Do not call it quits because you can accomplish this!

ALLEVIATE THE FEELINGS YOU HAVE REGARDING WORKING FROM HOME.

With TV, the Internet, and social media as continual aspects embedded in our behaviors, it would be probable to have preconceived notions about working from home. Many of the feelings regarding working from home are not exactly correct. Count on tough work and commitment to achieve the objective of working from home. However you assess it, an effectual and dynamic self-starter will do well at working from home. If you are unable to label yourself as dynamic and effectual right now, do not agonize. Those characteristics are fostered and you have to develop yourself to become effective.

Take a field trip. When you get tired of working in your office, take a trip to the living room or deck and enjoy your new surroundings. I like to plan to work at a coffee shop two times a week. This way, I have some great coffee and a change of scenery.

While working from home starts with a quest with yourself, there is the material aspect which would be just as critical. While your mind is in an appropriate place, you really have to work the material steps. Those tips are so critical because that concentrates upon the material aspect of working from home.

There are some specific habits which will prepare you for the experience. You need to plan to spend considerable time planning to telecommute from home. Before this planning starts, you need to be following the above suggestions. A habit involves a moment to place ideas into action. That starts with a pledge in mind. Keep a notebook to document the progress and that will encourage you to continue to stay on track. I use the Passion Planner for this. Write down ideas that you find are effective in keeping you on track. Try out new methods of getting your work completed. Chances are you will be constantly changing what you do until you find the schedule and techniques that work for you.

If you fall off track, get right back on. Working from home is a quest, and periodically folks fall off track. The critical thing is to bounce right back! Most importantly, make sure that you're enjoying your experience. Anyone who aspires to work from home expects to get some creative enjoyment from it. Furthermore, feed off the recognition you get along the way while you ultimately avoid traffic and long office meetings!

TAKING THE PLUNGE

There are many strategies that people use to work from home. At this point, you should know that planning is vital to being successful. If you are searching for the best technique to work from home, then be sure to allow yourself enough time to discover it. Once you do, schedule ample time to research and read up on effective tips and strategies. Agreeably, a few weeks to a month is a realistic period of time to reach that goal.

You are now completely ready to jump into the task at hand. However, first we will go over a few beneficial habits. That way you are as primed as possible for the moment you work from home. The three activities that you ought to do to get ready to work from home are: establish work routines, block out distractions and organize a workable schedule and workspace. Together these tips make a dependable core for your preparations.

Then for the time that you designate to prepare for working from home, focus on setting up work space, arranging a daily work schedule, and using productivity tools. The main issue that many will make when attempting to work from home is ignoring planning. Now that you are aware, make sure to designate no more than one month of planning before working from home.

When you disregard these actions, you will forego enjoying a work space that promotes productivity, having a clutter free area to work in, and enjoying an environment in which things can get done. Those results all come from the planning phase.

If you would invest in telecommuting from home, then you would find that it is shockingly easier than you may anticipate. Proper planning trains you to be totally ready. That results in enjoying an environment in which things can get done, having less stress to meet deadlines at last minute and having less job stress overall. These results guide you to actually work from home productively. That being said, do not solely dart through the preparations because all these results are just as critical.

Many will mistakenly believe that it could be tough, or even unfeasible to be a productive telecommuter. Realistically, it just takes someone who is determined and energetic to mentally and physically go through the preliminary steps. If you would entirely commit to refusing short-cuts in the period of preparation and perform the work necessary, then you are properly positioned to work from home.

It might look like a very long time to put in; however, spending a few weeks to a month tends to fly by. It would be natural to feel that way, especially when preparing for an experience as large as working from home. Provided you proceed to put in the appropriate effort, you will be working from home in no time. Working from home will be tough. However, through preparing the right way, you will be sure to conquer it and reap the rewards!

In every kind of business, proper management practices ARE truly important. As mentioned earlier, a virtual office also has its pitfalls.

KEEP YOURSELF ONLINE AS MUCH AS POSSIBLE.

Communication is very important if you work remotely. Most of us bring smartphones or tablets wherever we go, and you can take advantage of these technologies for your business. If you think a laptop is quite bulky, consider a hybrid laptop. Which brand you should buy? If you don't have any idea for now, check out CNET's post on the best hybrid laptops of 2015.

For easy surfing while on the road, Wi-Fi is the most common internet connectivity. In case you need an alternative, you can use an EV-DO or Evolution Data Optimized card. It's the same as 3G and works as a digital modem for your phone to your computer. I use a Verizon box for I do not like paying hotel internet charges and like to always have a backup.

MANAGE YOUR TIME WISELY.

Time management is always an issue for people working remotely. You can manage your time wisely by discipline. You have to set schedules and follow them. Track the time you spend on the computer. You can take advantage of time-tracking apps like Time Doctor.

COLLABORATE WITH YOUR TEAM MEMBERS.

If you work with spreadsheets and documents, Google Drive is the best option for you. Or if you're more into project management, Basecamp is a good choice. It lets you collaborate on documents and assign tasks.

BE PROFESSIONAL.

Respect your work as if you're still working from an office. Watch your behavior. Are you disciplined? If not, it's time to find a job and leave the comfort of your own home. There are many fish in the sea. The virtual market continues to expand and the next thing you know, your virtual office business is failing. So before you reach that point, motivate yourself a little more. Always remind yourself that time is money. High self-motivation is required in this kind of business.

SET UP A SCHEDULE.

Working on an uncompromised schedule makes you feel like you're working on regular hours. Doing this will also boost your productivity as your body gets used to the habit of working on a specific time.

CHILDPROOF YOUR HOME OFFICE.

Safety is an important consideration in having a home office when you have children in the home. Secure the cabinets and drawers and keep your office tidy.

SET UP REWARDS.

It can be "time-off" or benefits you can get after working hard. I like what Laura Vanderkam does to reward herself—she gets herself some sushi and a glass of Chardonnay. I'm no fan of sushi, but I like the idea of indulging myself with something after a tedious task. There are other frugal ways to reward yourself such as reading a book, or give some time to your favorite hobby. If you want a better reward for a bigger accomplishment, getting out of town won't hurt.

TAKE A BREAK.

Do you feel stressed and irritated for no apparent reason? Maybe it's a sign that you need to take a break from work. Whether it's an evening out or taking longer lunch breaks, you have to set aside time for you.

Working from home takes a lot out of any person. Unfortunately, every individual does not really possess what it takes. There are some definitive strategies that work more powerfully than others to ensure that you are unfailingly training for your objective the right way. Recognizing this will guide you to ultimately work from home successfully.

Typically, a person who tends to be distracted or disengaged might not be really productive when working from home. They would maintain the characteristics of someone who answered no to the following question:

DO YOU MANAGE TIME EFFECTIVELY?

If you wish to work from home, some characteristics are required. Being motivated would be an actual must. If you wish to accomplish your aspiration of working from home and ultimately be a productive worker, then you would need to be determined to meet your daily and weekly and monthly goals.

The secret to being a success at working from home would be to plan in advance, and also to complete the steps in your scheduling. Any person can declare that they want to work from home. Additionally, pretty much anybody can succeed at working in an office. However, telecommuting is surely beyond that. The time to concentrate on tactics come in the preparation stages. As with many activities in life, if you desire to do well, then make sure you prepare.

Establishing work routines is a vital strategy in getting ready to work from home. However, people usually ignore the importance of that. The truth remains that establishing work routines is absolutely necessary. On a different note, working from home also serves additional aspects of our everyday lives.

Blocking out distractions might be a no-brainer because that would be vital for overall success while you work from home. Blocking out distractions would be critical when you telecommute from home simply because of what is necessary to meet deadlines.

Lastly, organizing a schedule and workspace is vital to be certain you are productive in working from home. It might look like an effortless step, but it is not unheard of to waver from it. Therefore, continue organizing a useful schedule and workspace while maintaining concentration on living out your aspiration.

The strategies to working from home serve not only the aspiration of telecommuting from home, but each step truly brings a plethora of benefits which will complement other aspects of your life. It's straightforward to see that enjoying a work space that promotes productivity is not just a great benefit to working from home, but also for life in general. Likewise, spending less time on work and more time with family or friends is commonly known to serve different areas of life. Even finishing daily work in fewer hours will be beneficial outside of working from home. Other than being a productive, some people will appreciate how working from home improves their lifestyle in general.

The moment you integrate the tactics in order to work from home, you will find that your working attitude has greatly improved. Any effectual person will become even more effectual. Any dynamic person will be even more dynamic. And the energetic person will be even more energetic. That is why there's no better opportunity to get started than today!

Chapter 5: It Is Your Work Space

A guide full of things to accomplish before working from home would rapidly fill up several full-length books. Working from home is tough. It is clearly reflected by the large amount of coaching material convenient to individuals aiming to telecommute from home. Despite this fact, there are some key tips which any successful telecommuter ought to make to their regimented schedule. It also does not matter how experienced you are; you can make it work. The most critical aspect to keep in mind is that you need to prepare, both physically and mentally.

Setting up work space would be the key of any routine. You would never be ready to work from home if you just work amid the hustle and bustle of your family around you as you work from the kitchen counter. Find a space that gives you a place to keep you away from distractions and noise. Set up a regimented schedule and stick to it. It would be acceptable to take some time off every now and then, but you need to stay fairly focused with your schedule and work space every day. You will start to think differently, become more creative, and enjoy what you are doing.

You will be better primed for stumbling blocks because they will happen. However, keep your goal of being productive consistently on your mind. . Remember that you are an effective person, and you need to make the necessary changes to reflect that. Get in the practice of setting up work space so you are constantly enjoying a work space that promotes productivity and having a clutter free area to work in.

Equally critical as setting up work space would be arranging a daily work schedule. When you observe people who have productively worked from home, you will see that they constantly arrange a daily work schedule. It is because they perceive the importance of this practice. Arranging a daily work schedule results in spending less time on work and more time with family or friends. It is commonly known that arranging a daily work schedule also help you meet short- and long-term goals. Plan your next day the night before. By having a plan for the next day, you will stay on track and be more focused. This could save you time, and we all know that free time is one of life's greatest rewards.

Many people would agree that they could be having less stress to meet deadlines at last minute solely by arranging a daily work schedule. That will get your mind focused on coordinating your everyday activities to work from home. When telecommuting, being productive and time efficient should encourage you to keep in mind why you are doing this to begin with. You also should remember the tips and methods that have assisted you before.

Another great benefit that a successful telecommuter has is that they use productivity tools. They finish daily work in fewer hours. Being ready to work from home swiftly is important. Using productivity tools has a multitude of beneficial effects which go beyond telecommuting from home. Using productivity tools results in finishing daily work in fewer hours as well as meeting deadlines easier and quicker.

There are a few additional considerations to keep in mind while you are using productivity tools. Make use of timesaving apps. It will directly yield a more positive result to saving time while working and this will allow you more free time. Furthermore, using productivity tools will encourage you to have less job stress. And through developing a positive point-of-view, it'll serve you with any discouraging moments you may experience. Think about what you could make happen to enhance your decisions, and move on from there. An enthusiastic point-of-view will make all the difference while you are working from home.

CLASSIC MISTAKES MADE AS YOU WORK FROM HOME

Surely, there are a few activities that you'll not want to attempt when telecommuting from home. While any new successful telecommuter might make certain slips, there are a couple in particular that you would want to avert at all costs.

Do not start the day without a plan. It will cause you to backpedal in your best efforts. Why would someone put in all that sweat just to reverse what they have done? That is what takes place when you start the day without a plan.

There's something that will help you avert certain mistakes from developing. If you've been telecommuting from home for some time, set some time off to break up the day.

Additionally, do not put off your morning ritual. It would be the other critical issue that any successful telecommuter ought to avoid. While there are several tips to successful telecommuting from home, following these tips will yield a beneficial ending no matter what. Provided you are smart with your activities and pursue being the most effective employee, then you are ready to telecommute.

Now that your virtual office is up and running, you have to keep it organized for it to be a more productive place to work in. There's an old adage I like to adhere to is "There is a place for everything and everything in its place." There are many blog posts and self-help articles about home office organization. I personally like Martha Stewart's tips on desk organization. I like the idea of having personalized items such as tins and paper weights as well as erasable labeled drawers.

If you're a fan of labeling stuff, I think you should take a look at Toni Hammersley's home office, which was posted at A Bowl Full of

Lemons. She has a PC connectible labeling system which can be bought from Amazon at $70.

I also came across Diane Albright's tips on decluttering a workspace. I like her concept of getting your desk in order one hour before closing time. Well, to give you more of that, here are 10 things you might want to include in your home office for it to look more organized:

Floating shelves. There are lots of shelves as well as floating ones at Ikea and Home Depot. But you can make one for yourself, too. Do you want to know how? If you want a simple floating shelf, you can find one here. And another one here from Wikihow. These DIYs are easy to follow as long as you have the right materials since they provided some images.

A pegboard might also work for you. If you want some ideas, maybe you can check out these examples from Apartment Therapy. As you'll see from the pictures, there are lots of additions to the desks and crafts rooms. You may not include all the ideas, but you will surely find some that could work if you want a more-organized work space. Or if you want an alternative with pegboard, you can make your own memory board for your notes. Want some ideas for memory board? Go check out some photos from Houzz.

Large bins or boxes can also be useful. It is possible to recycle your old paper boxes by spraying some paint and adding some embellishment like jewelry and crystals. I like Jen of I Heart Organizing blog's ideas on DIY storage boxes.

Binders. Staples has some colorful binders which you can use for your own home office.

Hanging containers are great for holding markers, sharpies, and pens.

File folders. Many of us still believe in the old philosophy of saving everything including all types of incoming bills and invoices. I think the new philosophy is better: decide what to keep and what to shred. Scanning and keep digital copies takes   up very little space.

Wall file. The Container Store has some cute and beautiful wall files which are available in brocade designs. Ikea also has some wall file holders with matching magazine file boxes.

Magazine rack. An old ladder can turn into a beautiful magazine rack just like this.

A USB hub. Want a homemade USB hub? You can get inspiration from this YouTube video.

Wall manager. These can also be done easily as long as you have all the needed materials such as cardboard, old stationery, an old tray, and a magnetic board.

If you want cool items in your home office, here are some examples:

> ➢ A USB cup warmer
> ➢ Waterproof keyboard
> ➢ Spy Pen video camera
> ➢ Humidifier

D.H. Vincent

Chapter 6: Keep in mind

As we have recently explored, working from home takes quite a bit out of any person. These home workers should be effectual, dynamic, as well as energetic. Many people might have these attributes: however, the truth is that preparing for an experience as impacting as working from home might truly strip those wonderful attributes away from you. Below are a handful of procedures you ought to apply that will help you nurture these attributes.

Priming for working from home takes some energy. Most of these strategies will be ingrained in your brain during this process. Since you will likely be investing an amount of on planning, you should have enough time to dedicate your energy on these rules.

Just create an environment that is conducive to your working style. This is especially practical while you are setting up work space, because being comfortable while you work is key to being productive. This is not the only great benefit that following this rule will bring. Also, having a clutter free area to work in and enjoying an environment in which things can get done are additional benefits which also bring the most noticeable outcome.

Also, plan your next day the night before. This rule is not an option. By having a plan for the next day, you stay on track. If you consider yourself a competent worker, then do not leave your desk until you have planned the next day's routine.

You need to unfailingly have your focus concentrated on using productivity tools. These tools help you to be more focused while you work, and that is absolutely worth it. The tools will help you finish daily work in fewer hours. Just make use of timesaving apps and tips. This will free up time and they will enable you to eventually meet deadlines easier and quicker.

Working from home is not like working in a remote office. While anybody can try to telecommute from home, it takes someone who's energetic and effectual to really reach this objective of working from home.

The moment you are entirely serious, you can accomplish anything! Think back to the below questions:

Do you manage time effectively?

Are you able to prioritize your tasks?

Are you self-motivated?

When you work from home, these characteristics will serve you. If you heed these main rules, and you set up work space, arrange a daily work schedule, and use productivity tools, then you will be a productive telecommuter in no time!

BUILDING RELATIONSHIPS

Building relationships in a virtual environment is like being in a complicated long distance relationship. You haven't met the person face-to-face but you have to trust and communicate with each other for the sake of your business.

It feels out of touch to be with members you haven't met. Unlike the traditional work space, you can easily get along with team members with water cooler effect or informal conversations. How are you going to do that in a cyberspace work environment?

SHARE A BIT OF SOCIAL AND PERSONAL EXPERIENCES.

We're lucky that we have technology which we can use to build relationships among virtual teammates. You can be creative using podcasts to share our stories. Technology also gives us an opportunity to introduce ourselves through audio or video recordings.

ENCOURAGE CONVERSATIONS AMONG YOUR COLLEAGUES.

Be proactive in having some informal conversations with your teammates. Remember, humans are social animals. It's easy for us to assume the worst if we don't know what others are up to.

BE AWARE OF CULTURAL DIFFERENCES.

Because your team members are based around the globe, you also have to be aware of some cultural differences. For example, sending very short and straightforward emails is normal to some countries but for some, a longer one shows more politeness.

BE PRESENT.

Don't make your colleagues feel you're absent. Being present means being available to your teammates. Informal chats will allow you to be more familiar with your team and a start to establishing trust.

TREAT TIME ZONES FAIRLY.

Your teammates may be located across many time zones. These time zone differences can be one challenge for the team. Thus, you need to be proactive in overcoming these time barriers. You can do this by rotating your meeting schedule.

Once you commit to working from home, there are many activities that you can do to telecommute from home better. Here are a handful of tips which will end in working from home:

- Setting up work space has already been discussed in full detail, and that would be rather critical while you are working from home. Please be sure that you are comfortable while you work. Furthermore, make it a habit to create an environment that is conducive to your working style. That does not just affect working from home, it actually is applicable to your lifestyle in general.

- You should know that arranging a daily work schedule would be essential as well. It might get tough to make everything happen on your own as you go. Therefore, a great technique to having a plan for the next day keeps you on track. Always plan your next day the night before. This will allow you more motivation to arrange a daily work schedule as you prepare to work from home.

- It might seem tough to stay focused on using productivity tools, though it is critical for the objective of working from home. It is beneficial to make use of timesaving apps. This will result in higher productivity and give you more free time.

Working from home will allow you to reap positive results, especially as more time passes. When you work from home, you might experience the following results:

- Bear in mind enjoying a work space that promotes productivity will happen more as long as you not only set up a good work space, but clean up debris at the end of the day.

- Setting up a work space will equally help you have a clutter free area to work in.

- Arranging a daily work schedule will result in spending less time on work and more time with family or friends.

- Furthermore, arranging a daily work schedule helps with meeting short- and long-term goals.

- Through preparing to work from home, you should be using productivity tools and will finish daily work in fewer hours because of it.

- Using productivity tools also will meet deadlines easier and quicker.

Telecommuting from home entails doing all of these preparations and celebrating the results that follow. Furthermore, following are a handful of additional tips:

- Most timesaving apps are reasonably priced and have lifetime usage benefits. Create separate lists of your tasks for work and for household chores. This works especially for moms. If you want to master your to-do list, it is important that you find

- Chew gum. They say chewing gum boosts productivity. Some say it is just a myth. But one study in St. Lawrence University in New York suggested that chewing gum has positive cognitive effects. Whether it is proven to boost productivity or not, chew a stick.

- Place a plant near your desk. Plants, when placed strategically, raises alertness by up to 70%. Some good choices are areca palms, which humidifies naturally; variegated snake plant, which purifies the air; and lemon balm which elevates one's mood.

Working from home takes a great deal of effort. Fortunately, if you use the encouragement offered here while you telecommute, then you will be more than ready by the end of your planning period to give your at-home job your very best work and attention.

Though remember, these suggestions are solely a starting point. The moment you are completely done reading this information, you would perceive what is required to work from home. Use these observations to become more positive, and you will be prepared in no time.

THE BEST SYSTEM FOR WORKING FROM HOME

There are heaps of methods convenient to individuals thinking about working from home, and they all declare to be the best. In fact, a few of these methods, which you might find online, ensure some good positive results. Nonetheless, the victory of working from home depends upon each person as well as his or her point-of-view towards preparing and carrying it out. A great successful telecommuter will be a great successful telecommuter no matter what the situation. Likewise, a bad successful telecommuter will continue to get worse despite and contine to work from home as an amateur if he or she fails to continue to improve in using the advice given. Working from home is a mental activity just as much as it could be a physical one. Continue to update your process and methods of being productive.

During the planning period leading up to this big moment, you might get fairly busy preparing in advance. Not only will telecommuting from home physically challenge you, but also it equally stimulates your intellect. In regards to preparing the general strategy, multi-faceted ongoing planning is surely critical. There are heaps of tools at your disposal to help see the specifics of working from home. However, your individual intuition must be a better alternative than any tool. After all, you perceive your body and mindset like no one else. Use that know-how to calculate your target and do not doubt your intuition because it is not likely to wrongfully guide you.

We determined that the normal period of time someone trains to work from home is up to a month. Therefore, you need to be generous when preparing your time. Do the math and determine the time you would need. Lastly, adjust your goals accordingly and dig in.

During the time you prepare to work from home, you might find additional people who are attempting to accomplish the same objective. Also consider, they're likely working with a different timeframe than you. Therefore, do not get caught up competing with their timetable or methods if it does not work with your natural rhythm. That is precisely how many people get frustrate and ultimately give up. You've recently begun the first big step. Therefore, keep going at your own pace.. Start out slowly and gradually and take more time to research the possibilities as the preparations progress. That will ensure that you would be totally primed to work from home.

While these strategies described here are not foolproof, they're the ideal starting points for newbies attempting to work from home. There are absolutely many tips that you can accept to fit into your period of preparation, since you know your mindset. Use this know-how, as well as the plan set forth to jump out there and ultimately work from home! If you are smart with how you schedule your time, and fully apply all of the details here to calculate a solid strategy, then you will be a great successful telecommuter in no time!

D.H. Vincent

Chapter 7: Do's and don'ts

Any idea of working from home may be stimulating as well as intimidating. Being productive would be a large enhancement in any successful telecommuter's regime. Initially, that may look impossible. Nonetheless, with the appropriate briefing and foresight, working from home can be mastered by anyone. Just like any taxing challenge, working from home might be mastered in a multitude of ways. These are a few things which any successful telecommuter must (and must not) think of:

BEFORE WORKING FROM HOME

While the challenge is working from home, there could be many considerations which any successful telecommuter ought to accomplish beforehand. That will ensure that working from home is not an overwhelming challenge.

DO ESTABLISH WORK ROUTINES

If you want to work from home, you will be investing sufficient time preparing. That will physically encourage you to finish daily work in fewer hours and meet deadlines easier and quicker.

DON'T START THE DAY WITHOUT A PLAN

It can be easy to neglect giving your mind some time off from briefing. However, this day of leisure trains the mind to think of the aspiration of working from home. Grant your mind some time to think of accomplishing your goals so you avoid exhausting yourself.

DO Block Out Distractions

The preparation stages to working from home is critical and by reflecting this effortless guideline of blocking out distractions, you will be carrying out what you could to prepare.

DON'T Put Off Your Morning Ritual

If you miss any milestones in the root of the preparations, they should not adversely affect the general objective provided you take the effort to bounce back on track.

While Working From Home

DO Set Up Work Space

Recognize what you can achieve. Set your objective appropriately. By reflecting this guideline, you will enjoy a work space that promotes productivity and have a clutter free area to work in. Additionally, you will also enjoy an environment in which things can get done.

DON'T Make Your Tasks Too Large To Do At One Sitting

The most experienced successful telecommuter are ready to work from home faster. That would be because they have personal experience. Reclaim your energy and avoid analyzing yourself with a different successful telecommuter and compare your progression only with yourself.

DO Arrange a Daily Work Schedule

This is an essential guideline. By following this guideline in your regimen, you will enjoy a work space that promotes productivity as well as have a clutter free area to work in. Furthermore, you will enjoy an environment in which things can get done.

DON'T Worry About Failure

If you find your plan is not working, adjust it. Research new methods. Try new ways to be productive.

AFTER WORKING FROM HOME

After preparing to work from home, remember, the quest is not totally fulfilled! Here are a few do's, as well as don'ts, to remember once you achieve this goal:

DO Be Sure To Take Time to Enjoy Your Favorite Hobbies, Activities, and Pastimes

DON'T Fail To Take Some 'Me' Time

DO Take Some Time to Exercise

DON'T Omit Rewarding Yourself

These are certainly pretty easy tips to reflect. These are certain pretty easy tips to reflect while working from home. Realize this quest and keep in mind that the quest is yours!

D.H. Vincent

Chapter 8: Oh, the changes you will see

Working from home is not for quitters. It can be incredibly tough and the task does not get easier. Nonetheless, if you will brave this task to the end, you may find you are not the same kind of person that you had been before you started. No matter how well you prepare, something relating to merely attempting to work from home gives so many direct benefits.

For example, you learn how to work from home. Whether you flourish or fail, understanding how to prepare would be valuable to know. Regardless of the wealth of encouragement and knowledge which you can find online or in productivity books, attempting to work from home gives special insights into what degree the various strategies work. That sort of know-how not only results in understanding yourself better, but also gives you much required information for related endeavors.

Ultimately, working from home proves how completely devoted you are. Working from home would be a goal that several people maintain, but hardly a few maintain the dedication and focus to complete. Working from home proves your commitment through the eyes of other people and your paycheck, but also it proves it to your mind. The guts as well as the dedication it involves to perform telecommuting from home should only improve over time.

Working from home helps your intellect through showing you have what it takes to be self-motivated. Working from home also expands brainpower. The moment you work from home, you may be astounded by your progress in making it this far both mentally and physically. Oh, and do not forget the financial aspect. You will be feeling these benefits for lots of years.

Conclusively, working from home offers you bragging rights. So then, not only can you share the stimulating details of working from home with your friends, but you can share the stages of preparation. Also, you will learn what you are capable of. Working from home involves taking leaps of courage, as well as knowing you have what it takes to attempt something so life-changing.

Working from home certainly will be difficult and challenging, but it transforms you so many ways. It would be no shocking surprise that only certain people do well with working from home. You could be showing yourself and the world that you maintain the capabilities and know-how to attempt some bigger things in life! Being your own boss has its advantages.

WORKING FROM HOME - THE LIFESTYLE

It is immediately clear that people who strive to work from home come in numerous shapes and sizes. Nonetheless, no matter the skill level, there are certain considerations which are natural among the people who want to work from home. The reason heaps of people who work from home maintain success is because they maintain a lifestyle with comparable values. That does not mean they live parallel lives, because that would be impossible, and misguided. Most people who work from home come from numerous walks of life. While they might not share everything in common, there are certain lifestyle traits as well as tendencies that they all experience.

Obviously, these behaviors involve establishing work routines. Without that, working from home would seem impossible. Nonetheless, establishing work routines is not strictly tailored to just working from home. Furthermore, the behaviors involve blocking out distractions and organizing schedule and workspace. Telecommuting from home will require setting up work space as well as arranging a daily work schedule. The truth is that telecommuting from home would be an investment into the future. Furthermore, using productivity tools can lead to many kinds of positive results.

Because of that, a few people who want to work from home, especially those who are strong-willed, will immediately identify these extra benefits. Those results do not come exclusively from setting up work space, either. After putting forth so much effort in planning your everyday life to work from home, numerous people would notice themselves automatically making better everyday choices in other areas of life. Most people who have worked from home could find that they are more prepared to enjoy a work space that promotes productivity and have a clutter free area to work in. While that is not a miraculous talent that you will gain when you choose to work from home, that would be something which will gradually blend itself in your behaviors and your paycheck..

It can be really easy to be overwhelmed without even knowing it. If you maintain lots of friends who also would like to work from home, you may find that a few of them hardly concentrate on anything else but working from home. As with any behavioral choice, a little careful moderation would be required.

While writing this final chapter, I wondered why people are too obsessed with the idea of "work-life" balance. For me, it has become overrated. Personally, I don't buy into the phrase of work and life balance since these are two different things. Some say they should not overlap.

However, things could be different day by day like there are days when we do more work and there are days when we spend more time with our family. According to the Work Life Balance website, achievement and enjoyment are the front and back of the coin value of life. But we all have our own belief systems when it comes to success and happiness. For some, success in career matters more than anything else. But for many people, it is the quality of life that's more important.

It's because we all have values. These values are not the things we like to have but the things we need for us to be happy.

As a telecommuter, I believe I'm here in this situation because I chose to have personal freedom of how and where I work. If I were in the office, I would have the chance for a higher position. I would have some time for daily chit-chats with colleagues during breaks. And oh, I do miss coffee breaks! However, by being a telecommuter, I have more possibilities and control. If I want to visit family in another part of the country, I go with my laptop in tow.

Perhaps, it's not really about work and life but rather work and non-work. Or shall we say, "On" and "off" mode towards career because in the end, we all have personal lives. Here are some suggestions for you to have some time, not just for work, but also for other things that matter to you.

KNOW THE NATURE OF YOUR JOB.

Is the competition in your field very high that you have to work a little harder? Burning the midnight oil to excel in your field isn't bad at all. But if your work causes you too much stress, maybe it's time to think again why you worked that hard.

MANAGE YOUR TIME WISELY.

They say the most successful people never procrastinate. Even if you're an extremely busy person, you can do a lot in a single day with the right time management.

LEARN TO SAY NO.

Don't burden yourself with extra duties. As long as you get your task done, you can let it go. Sometimes, we think we need to impress our bosses a little more. But chances are we end up doing more tasks at work and they are not rewarded.

SPEND QUALITY TIME WITH YOUR FAMILY.

There's no sense in working more than 10 hours a day at home when you can't even be there for the children. Sometimes, it breaks my heart that being there for the kids does not always mean you're present or available for them.

Avoid working extra hours.

There are times when we can't help but work several hours more. It's all because of the fruits of our desire. We want better things in life, like a dream house or funds for education. But we often overlook the negative effects of working a few hours more. It can suffer relationships. Just imagine how your loved ones would feel if you can't be around on some important family gatherings.

D.H. Vincent

Conclusion

Working from home is no easy task, and sometimes individuals do not consider the things they would need to do to make it work. So much effort is spent on preparing, yet hardly a thought is given to the daily recovery strategy. While focusing on telecommuting from home is critical, you may want to also consider the things you need to pursue after your work day. There is no doubt you would feel more positive about yourself after achieving a good balance of work and fun.

COMMON QUESTIONS ABOUT WORKING FROM HOME

At this point, you might be mindful of the preparations you would take to work from home. If you have a question which hasn't been answered here, do not agonize. Here are three typical questions which come up regarding working from home:

Is it possible to work from home inexpensively?

Commonly, it would be possible to work from home for very little money. It would be overkill to put in heaps of money preparing to work from home. Following are a few suggestions to manage your wallet.

- Most timesaving apps are reasonably priced and have lifetime usage benefits. Create separate lists of your tasks for work and for household chores. This works especially for moms. If you want to master your to-do list, it is important that you find

- Chew gum. They say chewing gum boosts productivity. Some say it is just a myth. But one study in St. Lawrence University in New York suggested that chewing gum has positive cognitive effects. Whether it is proven to boost productivity or not, chew a stick and see.

- Place a plant near your desk. Plants, when placed strategically, raises alertness by up to 70%. Some good choices are areca palms, which humidifies naturally; variegated snake plant, which purifies the air; and lemon balm which elevates ones mood.

One other question which usually comes up while people are getting ready to work from home is regarding the typical "rules" to remember while telecommuting from home. Below are certain rules to keep in mind:

- While setting up work space, create an environment that is conducive to your working style. This would be to make sure you are comfortable while you work.

- Typically, arranging a daily work schedule would be critical when telecommuting from home. This would include having a plan for the next day to keep you on track.

- While you focus on using productivity tools, be sure to make use of timesaving apps. This will save time while working and allow you more free time.

Make sure to grant time to recover from each work day. If you are inexperienced at working from home, then it would be ideal to take it slowly. To minimize the time it would take to bounce back on track, here are some tips to help your mind recover.

After working from home, make sure to be sure to take time to enjoy your favorite hobbies, activities, and pastimes. You need to also make sure to take some time to exercise. It would physically help you recover a lot of the energy that you exerted during your work day. Additionally, be really careful not to fail to take some 'me' time.

After working from home, you may get burned out physically and mentally. After investing time planning your goals, it is natural to want a little rest. Take the time to do this. Promise yourself that work will be the last thing on your mind and let go. Let your hair down. Relax.

Now that you know what is expected to succeed when working from home, you also know who would not likely be effective. You know the characteristics that a productive telecommuter has, and now you can start the process of being your own boss in your own office.

Spending less time on work and more time with family or friends will help you realize that you do not know why you put this off for so long.

After putting forth time toward setting up work space and arranging a daily work schedule, you probably believe you are primed to work from home. No matter your feelings, make sure to test whether or not you actually are or if it is just your mind leading you to believe you are. Be on constant lookout for new ideas and strategies for productivity. Join social media groups and read blogs on keeping up on time-saving tools.

Make sure to devote some effort on using productivity tools. It's easy to overlook activities which are purposefully devoted for saving time. Nonetheless, through honing in your effort upon this particular purpose, you will find that you are able to finish daily work in fewer hours. Furthermore, using productivity tools trains you to meet deadlines easier and quicker and have less job stress.

You have already begun the first step toward working from home by reading about it. Most likely additional questions may come up, and a different way to do things might help you approach your goal in a more timely fashion.

Sometimes a "buddy system" would be a great solution when approaching a goal which requires a effectual and dynamic nature. While you would ultimately work from home by yourself, it is beneficial to join someone upon a parallel quest to talk about obstacles as they arise. Work at a local coffee shop and meet people doing the same thing you are. Be sure to pick like-minded companions and swap trade secrets.

For quite some time, the virtual office has become a solid option for many companies. It's because of its many benefits that could help both the employer and the employee.

But working in a virtual office also has its drawbacks , and these pitfalls usually take place with the kind of lifestyle we have. What's more important is that we can manage any drawbacks at work if we just take the time. Of course, it's important that we are aware of these disadvantages for us to know how to deal with them.

The viirtual office, no matter how challenging it seems, will be effective with the proper management of time and all other resources. We're lucky for having a plethora of tools and resources. Even if there are distance and time barriers, we can overcome them with the help of these tools.

A virtual office has some brilliant parts and some crappy parts as well. We've got to accept them and overcome them. I like what W. Clement Stone said about advantages and disadvantages:

"To every disadvantage there is a corresponding advantage."

Finally, I think a virtual office is every telecommuter's advantage. The idea of working anywhere sounds cool and is cool. It is rewarding on many levels. Being a telecommuter is truly a dream come true for me. I love that I can be in Europe or Florida or Chicago and not miss a beat in my career.

Are you ready to telecommute?

Thanks for reading! I hope you had a great time.

My best wishes to you on becoming a successful telecommuter!

Thank You!

I hope you enjoyed my book on planning to become a successful telecommuter.

Deb

Thank you for purchasing this book. If you are a telecommuter or want to be one, be sure to follow me on social media and on my website.

Web Site: http://www.dhvincentcom

D.H. Vincent

About the Author

D.H. Vincent is a lecturer and champion of creative thought towards solving life's challenges. Dr. Vincent is an online professor, writer, and an advocate of self education and addresssing difficult life situations with a winning response.

For more information on D.H. Vincent, please join her at http://www.dhvincent.com

www.ingramcontent.com/pod-product-compliance
Lightning Source LLC
Chambersburg PA
CBHW070848180526
45168CB00002B/997